11-14

D0601795

CREATING SCIENCE FAIR PROJECTS

WITH COOL NEW DIGITAL TOOLS

SUSAN HENNEBERG

rosen publishing's
rósen
central

NEW YORK

MONTROSE HIGH SCHOOL LIBRARY
320 SO. 2ND ST.
MONTROSE, CO 81401

Published in 2014 by The Rosen Publishing Group, Inc.
29 East 21st Street, New York, NY 10010

Copyright © 2014 by The Rosen Publishing Group, Inc.

First Edition

All rights reserved. No part of this book may be reproduced in any form without permission in writing from the publisher, except by a reviewer.

Library of Congress Cataloging-in-Publication Data

Henneberg, Susan.
Creating science fair projects with cool new digital tools/Susan Henneberg. — First edition.
  pages cm. — (Way beyond PowerPoint: making 21st-century presentations)
Includes bibliographical references and index.
ISBN 978-1-4777-1836-0 (library binding) — ISBN 978-1-4777-1847-6 (pbk.)
— ISBN 978-1-4777-1848-3 (6-pack)
1. Science projects—Juvenile literature. 2. Presentation graphics software—Juvenile literature. I. Title.
Q182.3.H466 2014
507.8'5–dc23

                                    2013023157

Manufactured in the United States of America

CPSIA Compliance Information: Batch #W14YA: For further information, contact Rosen Publishing, New York, New York, at 1-800-237-9932.

CONTENTS

INTRODUCTION

The science fair: what is your reaction to this annual event at your school? Do you groan with dismay, thinking of the hard work to come? Or do you look forward to the challenge of thinking like a scientist? There are many reasons to become involved in science fairs. You may be able to solve a real problem that can make this world a better place to live in. Science fair projects can teach you important skills, such as critical thinking and collaboration. They can spark your curiosity about how the world works. They can improve your science knowledge. They may also bring you awards and scholarships. Most of all, science fair projects can be fun.

Google employee Tom Oliveri told *USA Today*, "Science fairs help students to explore their vision and curiosity through science. Our company was founded on an experiment. We firmly believe that science can change the world." Sergey Brin and Larry Page created the Google search engine as a graduate school research project.

Science fairs have never been more important. Health, climate, and technology problems abound, calling for solutions. Teens all over the world have responded. In science fair projects, they have attacked breast cancer. They have improved

Google Science Fair grand-prize winner Brittany Wenger, seventeen, explains her research on breast cancer to President Barack Obama at the White House in 2013.

indoor air quality for people with asthma. And they have used algae as alternative energy.

Your parents may remember their science fair days. Their parents would drive them to the library to meet at a table with their friends. Librarians would pull down heavy encyclopedias. They would find dusty back copies of science magazines. Students would record data in spiral notebooks. They would present their projects on the familiar trifold cardboard poster boards that sat, row upon row, in the school cafeteria.

Welcome to the twenty-first-century science fair. While the scientific method never goes out of date, much about science fair research and experimentation has changed. Students have embraced the high-tech world of digital tools. Middle and high school students brainstorm in cyberspace using mind-mapping tools such as bubbl.us or Padlet. They use bookmarking and note-taking tools such as Evernote and Diigo to research their topics. Students accommodate their busy schedules by collaborating online with Google Docs. And they present their projects using digital screencasting and animation.

In the pages that follow, you will learn how to use these amazing digital tools to complete your own science fair project. You will learn a lot about science and how scientists work. You will gain important skills that will give you an edge in your future career. You might even do your own part to make positive changes in our world.

WHAT'S THE BIG IDEA? FINDING A TOPIC AND CRAFTING A QUESTION

Are you excited about beginning your science fair project? You should be. A lot of the cool technology you use was created by engineers whose curiosity was sparked by science fairs. Participating in science fairs will help you in many ways. You will become engaged in a real-world problem. You can use your creativity and critical thinking. And you will practice the twenty-first-century skills that will give you an edge in school and your career. Some of these skills involve using some great digital tools.

WHERE DO I START? THE SCIENTIFIC METHOD

Creating a successful science fair project starts with thinking like a scientist. What does that mean? All scientists use what is called the scientific method. These steps are the foundation of science research.

First, scientists are curious about a topic. They ask questions. Then they do some background research to learn about the topic. They focus on one important question. They construct a hypothesis, or an educated guess, that might answer the question. The next step is to test the hypothesis with an experiment. They collect data during the experiment. Afterward, they analyze the results. They draw a conclusion about whether their hypothesis was true. Finally, they report their results to other scientists.

STAYING SAFE USING ONLINE TOOLS

You will need to use your name, e-mail address, and perhaps other personal information when signing up for a digital tool. To stay safe and private online, however, you will need to follow some important rules.

The most important rule is to create a unique password. You need one that is impossible for someone to guess for each account. Try using the first letters in the words of a sentence you won't forget. Never share your password, even with a trusted friend.

Always check "private" in the settings menu. Make sure your computer has antivirus and security software. Be alert for phishing attempts, or efforts to try to hack into your accounts. Don't open e-mail from people you don't know. These tips will protect your safety and privacy online.

Let's try the steps with a real-world example. Eighteen-year-old Reno, Nevada, high school senior Mike Cruz loves to snowboard. He noticed that some of the trees along the highway to his favorite mountain ski resort were turning brown. They were also dropping needles. He wondered if it was because of the salt put on the road after a snowstorm. The salt melted the ice and prevented accidents. However, Cruz thought the salt runoff might be toxic to some varieties of pine trees. Other trees seemed to be fine.

Cruz wanted to enter his county science fair. He created an experiment with seedlings of different types of pine trees. He watered half with plain water. The other half were watered with salted water. He measured the growth of the plants weekly. Sure enough, his hypothesis was right. Some pine trees

An important part of any science experiment is taking complete notes on the changes you observe.

were still able to thrive with salted water. But others turned brown. He wrote a letter to the highway maintenance department about his concerns. He shared his results with his snowboarder friends on Facebook. He also began researching road de-icers that wouldn't kill plants. Is there anything in your life that causes you to wonder?

FINDING A TOPIC

You and your friends have decided to work on a science fair project together. You have to choose a topic. Where should you start? Brainstorming is a great method to generate ideas. And there are many cool digital tools to help.

Bubbl.us is a free, fun Web tool to use. After creating an account, you can make a concept map of your ideas. You might start with the different branches of science. For example, you may create a "parent" bubble with the word "physical science" in it. "Sibling" bubbles might include "biology" and "chemistry." Maybe you are interested in sports. This becomes a "child" bubble branching off physical science. You could generate ideas around basketball, softball, and swimming.

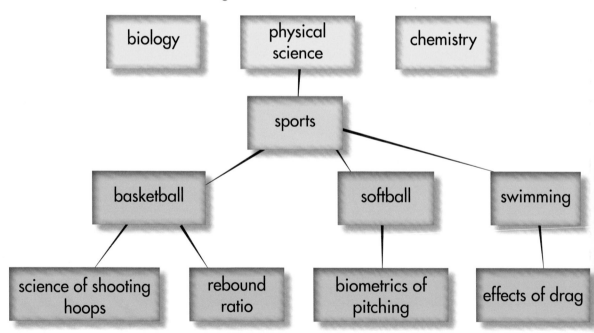

The power of brainstorming is to let ideas flow. One idea usually leads to another and another. Just add as many ideas to your bubble map as you can. You will eventually find one that clicks. You will move from very general ideas to specific topics that might be just right for your project.

Additional brainstorming programs include Mindomo and Padlet. All of these tools offer ways to make colorful, organized, and collaborative collections of your ideas.

CREATING A QUESTION

It probably won't take you and your friends long to find a topic. Then it is time to develop your question. Your experiment will answer the question. Science fair questions usually start with one of these terms: how, why, what, or when. For example, during brainstorming you might narrow a focus on "biology" to "food" and then to "fruit freshness." A question might be: "How does packaging affect the ripening of fruit?" To answer that question, you will need to do an experiment. It will involve testing various types of materials in which fruit may be packaged.

You may find many books in the library and sites on the Web that have ideas for science fair projects. You need to read through these with a critical eye. Many of them have fun models to build. Or they use chemicals to create flashy, attention-getting reactions. You can find instructions for building a

Students can win thousands of dollars in scholarship money for college by designing experiments that provide solutions to real-world problems.

camera in a box, a battery, or an electromagnet. However, these just show scientific principles. We already know how these things work. You want a real question that needs a real answer.

There are many important science questions you can try to answer in your science fair project. Hopefully, you can find one that impacts your world. Use the Internet to find topics about health, education, or the environment. Create shared concept maps to expand on your ideas. Post your ideas on blogs to see what response you get.

Digital tools will engage your mind in critical thinking. They will allow you to collaborate with your friends online. Today's students no longer have to find a time to physically meet together. You and your science fair group members can brainstorm, discuss your ideas, and choose a topic without leaving your own home.

RESEARCH: THE TREASURE HUNT

You found your science fair topic. You created a focused question. The next step is research. You need to find out all you can about your topic. You need to be able to share your findings with your group members. Then you need to collaborate to create a hypothesis. In a way, you will use your new knowledge to guess the answer to your question. Later, you will design an experiment. You need to find out if your answer is correct or not. But right now, it is time to go on a treasure hunt for information. Luckily, there are great digital tools to help you.

STARTING YOUR RESEARCH

Your first stop on your digital treasure hunt is your school or public library's databases. Many students rely on popular search engines such as Google to find information online. However, this is very limiting. All you see is the visible Web. Beyond these search engines is a vast wealth of other, more academic resources.

This treasure includes collections of scientific papers and journal articles in databases. Your school or public library may subscribe to these databases. You might need to get the password to access these collections. Once you do, you will find that the resources are more useful than search engine results. The resources are included in the databases because the information is trusted, accurate, and valid. That is important because science relies on accuracy.

One helpful database to use is findingDulcinea (http://www .findingdulcinea.com). This Web site calls itself "the librarian of the

Internet age." It has many Web guides that can provide background in different areas of science. Another database is Google Scholar. It collects academic articles. You can create a custom range of dates to make sure you get only current articles.

BOOKMARKING AND TAKING NOTES

Once you find information related to your topic, what do you do? Ten years ago, students might have printed out pages and pages of articles. Or they might have copied and pasted relevant text to word processing documents. They then e-mailed it to other group members. Now, however, there are easier ways to save and share information.

Note-taking from a variety of sources is an important academic and career skill. It can be helpful to bookmark good sources. There are many bookmarking tools on the Internet now. These allow you to save specific pages that might be useful. Some of them are known as social bookmarking tools. They let you share interesting Web sites with

Finding the information you need to solve a problem is an essential skill that will help you in college and in your career.

15

your friends. Some examples are Diigo, Zotero, and Zootool. Many of these sites have free versions. These typically have fewer features than paid versions. Others might need a subscription. You school may subscribe so that students can access them. Public libraries often have subscriptions, too. All you need to get started is a library card number.

You can put a tool on your Internet home page toolbar that allows you to bookmark a page with one click. You can add a description and a tag to your bookmarks. You can highlight certain sections of a Web page. You can even attach a digital sticky note that your teammates can read. This way, you can share your findings with them.

Diigo (https://www.diigo.com) is an example of a social bookmarking tool that allows you to organize and share your research with others on your team.

ORGANIZING YOUR NOTES

Bookmarking Web sites allow you to organize your notes. You can create different folders to hold them. One popular Internet tool to organize and share your research is Evernote. You can access Evernote on the Web from your computer, tablet, or smartphone. This handy tool allows you to organize your research into categories. For example, you might create one category for the history of your topic. You might create another category for an explanation of the science involved. A third category might be the notes you take during the experiment. Evernote can also store and organize the photographs you take of your experiment. By storing all this material on the Internet, everyone on the team has access to it.

FORMING YOUR HYPOTHESIS

Once you have done your research, it is time to form your hypothesis. It may be hard for you and your teammates to meet together in person. Now you can collaborate on the Web. One popular sharing site is Google Docs. This free service is part of Google Drive. You can open documents, type information in them, and share them with your team. All you need is a free Google account. Your teammates can add to the documents, making collaboration easy. Each of you can write about your understanding of your topic. Then you can propose your hypothetical answer to the question.

CONTROLLING VARIABLES IN EXPERIMENTS

Scientists often conduct an experiment to look for some kind of cause-and-effect relationship. They want to see if changes in one item cause a difference in something else. Scientists call the changing qualities variables. According to the nonprofit organization Science Buddies, "A variable is any factor, trait, or condition that can exist in differing amounts or types." Most experiments have three kinds of variables: dependent, independent, and controlled.

GOOGLE SCIENCE FAIR

The Google Science Fair is an online competition. It is for students between the ages of thirteen and eighteen from around the world. According to Google, the goal of the fair is to "look for ideas that will change the world." The deadline for submission of projects is usually the end of April. The prizes are amazing. Winners visit the Galapagos Islands on a *National Geographic* ship. They receive $50,000 in college scholarship money. And they can choose a hands-on experience at the headquarters of CERN (the European Organization for Nuclear Research), LEGO, or Google. One past winner investigated the effects of indoor air on asthma. Another looked at how different marinades for grilled meat cut down on cancer-causing chemicals. Another winner examined the role a phone app can play in testing for breast cancer. You can find more information at http://www.googlesciencefair.com.

When you conduct an experiment, the independent variable is the factor that you change. Then you observe what happens. You look at the dependent variable to see how it responds to the changes. The controlled variable must always be the same so that it doesn't affect the results.

Take, for example, Mike Cruz's pine tree experiment discussed in the first chapter. The dependent variable is the health of the pine tree seedlings. The controlled variable is the amount of water used for each seedling. It must be the same for all of them. The independent variable is the salt content of the water. Some water has salt in it. Some of it is plain.

Understanding how variables work will help you answer your science fair question. Your research will aid you in sorting out your variables. Finding good background material and organizing research notes used to be tedious work. Now, however, you can use online databases, bookmarking tools, and note-taking applications. This way, you can find and share your notes efficiently. Once you understand the science behind your question, you will be ready to find the answer.

TEST YOUR GUESS: CONDUCTING THE EXPERIMENT AND GATHERING DATA

For many students, conducting the experiment is the fun part. You and your teammates design and carry out an experiment that proves or disproves your hypothesis. You might be using natural materials such as plant life. You might be mixing chemicals, testing velocity, or writing a computer program. Many science fairs require you to keep a notebook. This documents your experiment. You may want to photograph or film the steps, too. Whatever you are doing, there are many cool digital tools to help. Here's how to start.

There are three main phases to conducting an experiment. First you need to find or construct the equipment needed. There are many experiments that use easy-to-find materials. Then you will actually do the experiment. This may take minutes, days, or weeks. You will need to record every step of the process. Finally, you'll organize and analyze your data.

THE FIRST STEP: SETTING UP YOUR EXPERIMENT

Setting up your experiment can be fun. For example, you might need to fill clay pots with potting soil. Or you might cut and fold paper airplanes. You may need to prepare plastic water bottles to hold stream water. Mike Cruz bought tree seedlings, pots, and soil. You might even use a computer for your experiment. One popular science fair topic is comparing people's reaction times to a stimulus. There are Web sites that use red and green lights to measure reaction times.

Your school's science labs may have the equipment you need to perform your experiment.

For some experiments you might need access to a laboratory. You might need microscopes, incubators, or centrifuges. Hospital or university labs may have researchers willing to mentor a student. You will need to be able to clearly explain your ideas about your experiment to a potential mentor. Your teachers may be able to steer you toward the right scientists to approach about your experiment. However, there are thousands of interesting science fair projects that can be done in your own home with everyday equipment.

USING VIDEO EDITING TO VERIFY DATA

Some science experiments may need to be accurately timed. For example, you might use a stopwatch to record the time it takes a homemade parachute to drop from the top of a ladder. However, some events happen quickly, within a few seconds. You may not be able to start and stop the time accurately. Here is where video-editing software can help. Set up a camcorder or smartphone to film the drop. Then use the slow-motion and freeze-frame features. They can help you determine exactly when an event started and stopped.

THE SECOND STEP: CONDUCTING THE EXPERIMENT

The second step is to conduct the experiment. It is important to record everything you do. A paper notebook or binder can work. However, think about keeping your notes in digital form. This will make them available to all of your group members and your teachers. Google Docs and Evernote are applications through which online documents can be shared. You will need to write the exact steps of the experiment, like a recipe.

You may want to set up video equipment to record your experiment and your procedures. It's a good idea to film everything you do. You can edit your video later. Then you can delete material you don't need. Some experiments may need weeks to develop. If this is your situation, you might just film when

Scientists—and science students—need to take accurate measurements when collecting the data to be analyzed in an experiment.

you take your measurements. For example, you might decide to sprout seeds in various mediums. You could film yourself measuring the height of the sprouts each day for three weeks. Other experiments might be filmed in one day. You could set up a camcorder to record yourself riding a bicycle with your tires at different pressures.

It is crucial to keep accurate measurements. Make sure you have the tools you need to do these measurements. Stopwatches, thermometers, tape measures, and scales are examples of scientific tools. Be clear about which measurement units you are using—for example, U.S. customary or metric units. You don't want to confuse inches with centimeters. A spreadsheet program such as Microsoft Excel or Google Sheets can be useful in recording measurements.

As an example, you may want to test a hypothesis that involves reaction times. There are many Web sites that can help with this. On one, a person clicks a button every time he or she sees a certain color. The Web site then reports the time it took in milliseconds. It is good science to repeat the experiment with a wide range of ages. You will also want to repeat the experiment several times per person. Setting up a spreadsheet to record reaction times is easy. Google Sheets will allow you to store the document online and share it with your group members.

SCREENCASTING YOUR EXPERIMENT

A fun way to document your experiment is to use a screencasting program such as Jing. Jing is a free application from TechSmith that allows you to capture images on your computer desktop. For example, you could use Jing to record a subject testing his or her reaction times. You can add text boxes, arrows, highlights, or captions to the images. If your computer has a microphone or you have one to plug in, you can narrate an explanation. With Jing, you are limited to five minutes per video. These videos are easy to share online. They can be e-mailed, placed as a link in Google Docs, or inserted into an instant message or Tweet.

Recording an explanation of your investigation adds a sophisticated touch to your project.

Snagit and Camtasia are more sophisticated programs made by the same company. They require purchase. However, they have special deals for educators and students. They also have free trial periods. A video of you updating your project notes could be a great supplement to your science fair notebook. A science fair judge might by impressed by your visible attention to the details of your experiment. The video records of your experiment will also be useful in the next step of the scientific process—analyzing the results.

WINDING UP YOUR PROJECT: ANALYZING DATA

It is now time to complete the last steps of the scientific process. You need to analyze your experiment data. You need to figure out if your experiment supported your hypothesis.

You probably have a lot of raw data that needs to be organized. Once that is done, you can evaluate the data. Then you can draw some conclusions. Did you get an answer to your question?

Scientists often organize their data into tables and use spreadsheet programs to do their calculations. They use graphs to display their results. Let's see how that is done.

ORGANIZING THE DATA AND DRAWING CONCLUSIONS

Many science experiments involve keeping track of trials. For example, students doing a reaction experiment would record data on the ages and genders of the people clicking on the green light. They would compile the data to see if the results supported their hypothesis.

Microsoft Excel has an easy AutoSum feature that can quickly calculate averages. You can choose "average" from the AutoSum drop-down menu. The data might look something like the table below. The table shows eight subjects. There were two subjects in each age group, one male and one female. Each subject did the experiment three times. The times are given in milliseconds.

	Trial 1 (ms)	Trial 2 (ms)	Trial 3 (ms)	Average (ms)
Male Ages				
10–20	200	190	195	195
21–30	160	155	150	155
31–40	174	172	170	172
41–50	195	190	185	190
Female Ages				
10–20	230	225	220	225
21–30	184	180	182	182
31–40	245	240	235	240
41–50	250	248	246	248

It is easy to draw conclusions from this table. The male in the age group twenty-one to thirty had the fastest reaction times among the men. Similarly, the female in that age group had the fastest reaction times among the women. How do you show this on a graph? A spreadsheet program such as Microsoft Excel or Google Docs can help. You can use the "insert" menu to turn your worksheet into a graph. Another resource is a graphing application such as Create A Graph from the National Center for Education Statistics (http://nces.ed.gov/nceskids/createagraph).

For this experiment, a line graph is best. Other graphs you might use for other experiments are bar or pie graphs. A scientific graph created from a spreadsheet would normally show the independent variable on the horizontal (x) axis. The dependent variable would go on the vertical (y) axis. These axes are the same ones you use in your math classes. In this case, the age of the participants would go on the x-axis. The time it took to click on the light would go on the y-axis.

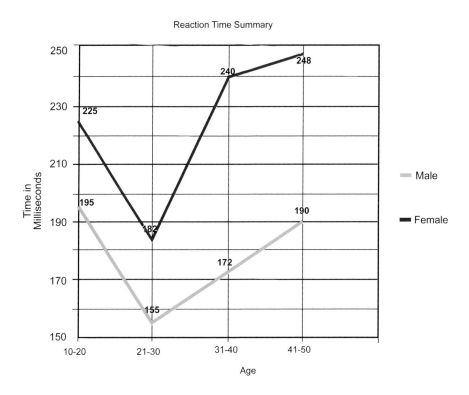

Reaction Time Summary

WRITING THE RESULTS

You will probably have to write up the results in a final report. You can collaborate with your team using document-sharing tools such as Google Docs. Your report will follow the steps of the scientific method. It should include your background material and your hypothesis. You need to explain the steps of your experiment. Then summarize your results. You need to state whether the results supported or contradicted the hypothesis. Finally, you should explain how the results of your experiment can be used.

Sometimes it can be confusing when several people are contributing to one document. One useful feature for Google Docs users is the revision history. Color-coded changes show who added to or changed the document. This is a good way to keep track of your collaboration.

MAKING A VIDEO OF YOUR EXPERIMENT

You might want to make a polished video of your experiment to include with your report. You may have taken video footage of your processes. There are several cool programs you can use to edit it. Students who have an Apple desktop or laptop computer can use iMovie to edit videos taken with a camcorder. Apps are available that allow video taken with an iPhone to be edited on the phone or on an iPad or iPod Touch. Students with PCs can also edit video taken with camcorders and smartphones. Windows Movie Maker is a free download from Microsoft. There are many affordable video-editing software programs from companies such as Adobe, Sony, and Corel.

You can add sound and video effects to your video. You will want to keep special effects to a minimum. This keeps your video looking professional. However, there may be times in which slow-motion may be appropriate. For example, students investigating oil spills may video the effects of substances that can absorb oil. Watching in slow-motion will help viewers understand what is happening. Students can use slow-motion to

Making a video of your experiment is a fun way to help the science fair judges understand your project.

explain the process to the science fair judges. Similarly, students may use a fast-forward or time-lapse technique to condense a long process into just a few minutes.

Once the video of your experiment is complete, you can create a DVD. Or you can upload the video to YouTube. The advantage of YouTube is that it is always available on any computer with an Internet connection. However, the Internet may not be available at your science fair. In that case, you can play the DVD using a laptop computer or a portable DVD player. Or you can save the video to a laptop or tablet computer's hard drive. Programs such

COOL TOOLS FOR CITING YOUR SOURCES

In order to cite your sources, you will probably create a bibliography to go with your science fair report. This means writing down all the information about the resources you used. You will need to use one of the major bibliographic styles, such as MLA (Modern Language Association) or APA (American Psychological Association). Your teacher will tell you what style to use.

Creating a bibliography can be confusing. However, there are some digital tools to help. Zotero (http://www.zotero.org) is a free online program that can help you with your references. It was created for advanced academic research. But it can help science fair researchers, too. It can work with your Web browser and word processing program to keep track of your sources. It can also create a bibliography in whatever style you need.

as Windows Media Player, Cyberlink Media Suite, or the DVD player on Apple products can play the video.

USING SOCIAL MEDIA TO GET FEEDBACK

Scientists in the real world often ask for feedback from their peers. It can be fun to see who might be interested in your project. Twitter can be a fast way of broadcasting your project to the world. If you are over thirteen, you can easily open a Twitter account. You can tweet a link to your video using the hashtag #sciencefair. Or you can add a post about your project to your Facebook account. This will add some adult professionalism to your social media presence. Instagram photos and Tumblr blogs about your project will also boost your academic credentials in cyberspace.

Chapter 5

SHOWING IT OFF: PRESENTING THE PROJECT

You finally reached the last step of your science fair project. Hopefully it's been fun. Maybe you caught your teammates on video, wobbling down the driveway on badly inflated bicycle tires. Or perhaps you watched your parents try to beat each other's reaction times. You carefully recorded data on detailed spreadsheets. You drew conclusions, created graphs, and documented your results. Now it's time to present your project to the world, or at least to the science fair judges.

ORGANIZING THE PRESENTATION

The presentation part of the science fair may make or break your chances of winning an award. You have to demonstrate that you understand the science behind your experiment. You have to show that you have con-ducted the experiment correctly. You have to effectively display the results of your different trials. And you need to explain your conclusions clearly. The twentieth-century way would have been to print out pages of text and graphs. Photographs would have provided visual records of the experi-ment. All of these would have been glued to a cardboard display board. Today, there are more exciting ways to show off your work.

The key to an effective presentation is organization. You need to tell the story of your project in a clear and engaging way. Here is an oppor-tunity to use creativity. Don't suffer from what many teachers call "end-of-project syndrome." Make sure that you have left enough time to put together your presentation. Judges will not reward last-minute work. This is the time to create a presentation that stands out from the rest. Your school might still use display boards. However, any student who has

A well-organized display supplemented with digital content may increase your chances of winning a prize at the science fair.

access to a laptop or tablet computer can add exciting digital content. Students at schools that require all-digital presentations have many opportunities to use cool digital tools.

THE PHYSICAL DISPLAY

Whether physical or digital, your presentation begins with good planning. If you are using a display board, the steps of your project should be presented in order. People read from top to bottom, left panel to right panel. Make sure the text is clear and error-free. Headings should draw attention to the steps of the project. First, design on paper where the typed explanations of the steps will be placed. Then print out the pages and arrange them.

Most science fairs allow students to include a multimedia device, such as a laptop or tablet computer. However, science fair judges seldom watch more than a few minutes of a multimedia presentation, so any audio-visual content needs to be short and to the point. It needs to complement the display board. It is not a substitute for it. For example, you may want to show a video of yourself conducting the experiment. This does not take the place of your lab notebook.

ADDING MULTIMEDIA CONTENT

What would be a fun way of providing multimedia content? One option is to use presentation software to make a slideshow of your project. The slideshow could tell the story of your project, step by step. It is easy to embed video footage of your experiment into software programs such as Keynote, Google Presentation, Prezi, or SlideRocket. You can include a link to your video, which you have uploaded to YouTube. Provide voice-over narration if you can.

All of these programs allow remote collaboration. The members of your team do not have to be physically together to create the product. At the science fair, you can set the audiovisual presentation to loop continuously during the judging period. This means that as soon as the presentation ends, it automatically begins to play again.

Instead of a narrated slideshow, another option is to

Students can take advantage of easy-to-use presentation software to add some excitement to their science fair projects.

make a short movie documenting your project. Start with the video footage you took of your experiment. Then add an introduction, discussion, and conclusion. You can edit the video using programs such as iMovie or Windows Movie Maker. The Google Science Fair, for example, requires students to submit a two-minute video summary or presentation as part of their project. Some of the presentations have embedded video. You can see examples of these videos and presentations at https://www.googlesciencefair.com/en/2013/previous-years.

Maybe you would like to include images or video footage of something you have created on your computer, such as a program. If so, screencasting tools can help. This approach is especially useful for students entering the computer science or engineering categories. Jing, for example, can capture

USING ANIMATION TOOLS

Adventurous students can kick their videos up a notch by using some great animation tools. GoAnimate is a free, easy, two-dimensional application. Students use drag-and-drop tools to animate premade characters. They can also create dialogue, and the application translates the script into speech. Voki is another free application. It allows users to choose avatars that can deliver sixty-second messages. You can choose your character and change its look. You can even choose an animal as an avatar. It might be fun to choose a squirrel to deliver a hypothesis about an environmental issue, for example.

screenshots. You can combine the screenshots into a narrated slideshow. Or you can record up to five minutes of video demonstrating your computer program or other computer work. You can upload and share your screencast at Screencast.com. This is a free hosting site for Jing content. You can also use Snagit or Camtasia if you need more than five minutes.

VIRTUAL SCIENCE FAIRS

All of these applications provide fun ways to add digital content to a live science fair. In addition, an increasing number of schools are requiring all-digital entries. For example, Hardy Middle School in Washington, D.C., began conducting all-digital science fairs in 2010. The Robert Goddard French Immersion School in Prince George's County, Maryland, is another school with a digital science fair. Other digital science fairs are the Google Science Fair, the U.S. Army's eCYBERMISSION for students in grades six through nine, and the Canada-Wide Virtual Science Fair.

For digital science fairs, a Web site can be a great way to show content. There are many free applications for building Web sites. Google Sites is part of the Google suite of applications. It integrates well with other Google content, such as Google Docs. Weebly is a student-friendly Web site program. It allows easy uploading of audio and video content.

Providing digital content will increase the audiovisual appeal of your project. You will also learn skills you can take to college and the workplace.

Over fifty years ago, scientists who wanted to collaborate created the Internet and then the World Wide Web to share science content. Since then, computer engineers have created thousands of digital tools. These amazing tools allow professional scientists—and budding scientists—to imagine, plan, document, and share their findings. Their products have truly made our world a better place. How will you use them to contribute to science?

GLOSSARY

APPLICATION A computer program that helps a user perform a specific function.

AVATAR A graphic image that represents a person.

BIBLIOGRAPHY A list of source materials used in the preparation of a work.

BLOG A Web site that contains a dated log of an individual's or group's opinions, observations, news, or information.

CITE To quote a source in support of a fact.

COLLABORATIVE Involving work with others on a joint project.

CONCEPT MAP A diagram that shows the relationship among various ideas.

DATABASE A collection of data organized digitally for convenient access.

EMBED To put something, such as video or graphics, into a computer program or Web page.

HASHTAG A word or phrase preceded by a hash mark (#), used to label a tweet for Twitter searches.

HYPOTHESIS A tentative explanation for certain facts or observations that can be tested with an experiment.

MENTOR An adviser, teacher, or guide, especially in a workplace or academic setting.

MIND MAPPING Using a diagram to visually outline information and show relationships among ideas.

PHISHING A fraudulent attempt to obtain financial or other confidential information from Internet users.

SCREENCAST A digital recording that captures the action taking place on a computer screen, often containing audio narration.

SPREADSHEET A worksheet in which data is arranged in columns.

STIMULUS Something that causes an activity or response.

VALID Having a scientific foundation; based on truth or logic.

VARIABLE Any factor, trait, or condition that can exist in differing amounts or types.

Canada-Wide Science Fair
1550 Kingston Road, Suite 213
Pickering, ON L1V 1C3
Canada
(416) 341-0040
Web site: http://cwsf.youthscience.ca
The largest extracurricular youth activity related to science and technology in
   Canada, the Canada-Wide Science Fair hosts the finalists from
   regional fairs around the country. It encourages an interest in science at
   all age levels.

Google, Inc.
1600 Amphitheatre Parkway
Mountain View, CA 94043
(650) 253-0000
Web site: http://www.google.com
Google says its mission is "to organize the world's information and make it
   universally accessible and useful." It has developed dozens of products
   to help students research, write, organize, share, and publish their
   ideas. It sponsors the Google Science Fair.

MediaSmarts: Canada's Centre for Digital and Media Literacy
950 Gladstone Avenue, Suite 120
Ottawa, ON K1Y 3E6
Canada
(613) 224-7721
Web site: http://mediasmarts.ca

MONTROSE REGIONAL LIBRARY
320 SO. 2ND ST.
MONTROSE, CO 81401

MediaSmarts is a Canadian not-for-profit organization for digital and media literacy. The goal of this organization is to teach children and youth the critical thinking skills they need to engage with media as active and informed digital citizens.

NASA Jet Propulsion Laboratory
California Institute of Technology
4800 Oak Grove Drive
La Cañada Flintridge, CA 91011
(818) 354-4321
Web site: http://www.jpl.nasa.gov/education/sciencefair
NASA Jet Propulsion Laboratory scientists provide videos, Web links, and resources to help young scientists create a winning science fair project.

Society for Science & the Public (SSP)
1719 N Street NW
Washington, DC 20036
(202) 785-2255
Web site: http://www.societyforscience.org
This organization hopes to inspire promising young scientists and engineers. It sponsors competitions for students, including the Broadcom MASTERS competition for middle school students and the Intel International Science and Engineer Fair for high school students.

WEB SITES

Due to the changing nature of Internet links, Rosen Publishing has developed an online list of Web sites related to the subject of this book. This site is updated regularly. Please use this link to access the list:

http://www.rosenlinks.com/WBPP/SciFa

Andrews, Georgina, and Kate Knighton. *100 Science Experiments*. London, England: Usborne, 2012.

Bonnet, Robert L., and Dan Keen. *46 Science Fair Projects for the Evil Genius* (Evil Genius). New York, NY: McGraw-Hill, 2009.

Dutton, Judy. *Science Fair Season: Twelve Kids, a Robot Name Scorch—and What It Takes to Win*. New York, NY: Hyperion Books, 2011.

Gardner, Robert. *Light, Sound, and Waves Science Fair Projects*. Berkeley Heights, NJ: Enslow Publishers, 2010.

Harris, Elizabeth Snoke. *Save the Earth Science Experiments: Science Fair Projects for Eco-Kids*. New York, NY: Scholastic, 2009.

Hock, Randolph. *The Extreme Searcher's Internet Handbook: A Guide for the Serious Searcher*. 4th ed. Medford, NJ: CyberAge Books, 2013.

Holland, Jim, and Susan Anderson. *Web 2.0 Hot Apps, Cool Projects: Science*. 2nd ed. Eugene, OR: Visions Technology in Education, 2010.

Jakubiak, David J. *A Smart Kid's Guide to Doing Internet Research* (Kids Online). New York, NY: PowerKids Press, 2010.

Mills, J. Elizabeth. *The Everything Kids' Easy Science Experiments Book: Explore the World of Science Through Quick and Fun Experiments*. Avon, MA: Adams Media, 2010.

Orr, Tamra. *Creating Multimedia Presentations* (Digital and Information Literacy). New York, NY: Rosen Central, 2010.

Randolph, Ryan P. *New Research Techniques: Getting the Most Out of Search Engine Tools* (Digital and Information Literacy). New York, NY: Rosen Central, 2011.

Vickers, Tanya M. *Teen Science Fair Sourcebook: Winning School Science Fairs and National Competitions*. Berkeley Heights, NJ: Enslow Publishers, 2009.

Walker, Pam, and Elaine Wood. *Computer Science Experiments*. New York, NY: Infobase Learning, 2009.

BIBLIOGRAPHY

Baugh, David. "Using iMovie in Science." CrunchEd Productions, October 22, 2010. Retrieved August 5, 2013 (http://www.crunchedproductions.com/?p=212).

Cruz, Michael. Interview with author. February 20, 2013.

Embi, Mohamed Amin. "Web 2.0 Sharing Tools: A Quick Guide." Scribd.com, 2011. Retrieved March 10, 2013 (http://www.scribd.com/doc/74330492/Web-2-0-Sharing-Tools-A-Quick-Guide).

"Hardy Middle School Digital Science Fair 6." Google Sites. 2011. Retrieved March 9, 2013 (https://sites.google.com/site/hardyms digitalsciencefair6).

Microsoft Safety & Security Center. "Teach Kids Online Security Basics." 2013. Retrieved August 5, 2013 (http://www.microsoft.com/security/family-safety/childsafety-internet.aspx).

National Association of Independent Schools. "A Global Paradigm Shift in Science Fairs." NAIS.org, April 9, 2007. Retrieved March 19, 2013 (http://www.nais.org/Articles/Pages/A-Global-Paradigm-Shift-in-Science-Fairs.aspx).

National Center for Education Statistics. "Create A Graph." NCES Kids' Zone. Retrieved March 19, 2013 (http://nces.ed.gov/nceskids/createagraph/default.aspx).

National Science Foundation, Office of Legislative and Public Affairs. "Fact Sheet: A Brief History of NSF and the Internet." August 2003. Retrieved March 19, 2013 (http://www.nsf.gov/od/lpa/news/03/fsnsf_internet.htm).

Open Education Database. "Research Beyond Google: 119 Authoritative, Invisible, and Comprehensive Resources." OEDb.org, April 2, 2013. Retrieved June 28, 2013 (http://oedb.org/library/college-basics/research-beyond-google).

Prince George's County Public Schools. "News Release: Robert Goddard
    French Immersion School STEM Fair Goes Virtual." January 17, 2013.
    Retrieved March 19, 2013 (http://www1.pgcps.org/communications
    /press.aspx?id=172114).

Schachter, Ron. 2011. "How Are Science Fairs Faring?" *District
    Administration*, October 1, 2011. Retrieved March 18, 2013 (http://
    www.districtadministration.com/article/how-are-science-fairs-faring).

Science Buddies. "Science Fair Project Ideas, Answers, & Tools." 2013.
    Retrieved March 19, 2013 (http://www.sciencebuddies.org).

Smoak, Ellen, and Robert Williamson. "A Student's Guide to Keeping the
    Science in Your Science Project." North Carolina Cooperative
    Extension Program. Retrieved March 19, 2013 (http://www.ag.ncat
    .edu/extension/programs/dte/science.pdf).

Society for Science & the Public. "Intel International Science and Engineering
    Fair." 2013. Retrieved August 5, 2013 (http://www.societyforscience
    .org/isef).

TeachingHistory.org. "Voki." 2013. Retrieved March 19, 2013 (http://
    teachinghistory.org/digital-classroom/tech-for-teachers/24655).

Vergano, Dan. "Google Unveils Global Science Fair Competition." *USA
    Today*, January 11, 2011. Retrieved March 5, 2013 (http://
    content.usatoday.com/communities/sciencefair/post/2011/01
    /google-unveils-global-science-fair-effort/1#.UWQOrhzrzCk).

Westchase District Community Portal. "A New Way to View a Science Fair."
    2013. Retrieved March 19, 2013 (http://ecommunity.westchase
    district.com/community/DisplayStory.asp?id=318&cid=16).

INDEX

ABOUT THE AUTHOR

Susan Henneberg has been a teacher at the high school and college levels in Reno, Nevada, for more than thirty years. She has also been a technology trainer for the Washoe County School District since 1995. Her Web 2.0 projects guide both students and educators in using the best of technology to increase productivity, accuracy, and enjoyment of their work. She hopes to inspire students to use science and technology to positively impact our world.

PHOTO CREDITS

Cover Martin Shields/Photo Researchers/Getty Images; pp. 4–5 The Washington Post/Getty Images; p. 9 Martyn F. Chillmaid/Science Source; p. 11 © AP Images; pp. 14–15 iStockphoto.com/Thinkstock; p. 16 www.diigo.com; p. 21 © Billy E. Barnes/PhotoEdit; p. 23 Martin Shields/Science Source; p. 25 © iStockphoto.com/mascough; pp. 30–31 Ingram Publishing/Thinkstock; p. 35 Jesse Bair/South Jersey Times/Landov; pp. 36–37 © The Star-Ledger/Andy Mills/The Image Works; cover and interior graphics (arrows) © iStockphoto.com/artvea.

Designer: Nicole Russo; Editor: Andea Sclarow Paskoff;
Photo Researcher: Amy Feinberg